POSTS:
EAD OF
FAKE NEWS

Stephen Currie

ReferencePoint
Press®

San Diego, CA

© 2018 ReferencePoint Press, Inc.
Printed in the United States

For more information, contact:
ReferencePoint Press, Inc.
PO Box 27779
San Diego, CA 92198
www.ReferencePointPress.com

LIBRARY OF CONGRESS CATALOGING-IN-PUBLICATION DATA

Name: Currie, Stephen, author.
Title: Sharing Posts: The Spread of Fake News/by Stephen Currie.
Description: San Diego, CA: ReferencePoint Press, Inc., 2018. | Includes
  bibliographical references and index. Audience: Grades 9 to 12 |
Identifiers: LCCN 2017025487 (print)| ISBN 9781682822982 (eBook) |
  ISBN: 9781682822975 (hardback)

CONTENTS

INTRODUCTION

Pizzagate

In late October 2016, shortly before the US presidential election, an astonishing rumor began circulating online. The story focused on Hillary Clinton, the Democratic Party's candidate for president, and it asserted that Clinton was kidnapping children and forcing them to work as prostitutes. "We're talking an international child enslavement and sex ring,"[1] read an October 30 tweet by a person using the name Carmen Katz. The story put Clinton at the center of the prostitution scandal but implicated other people as well, notably Clinton's husband, former president Bill Clinton, and her close adviser John Podesta. Most accounts also asserted that other Democratic Party leaders and government officials either knew about the prostitution ring or were involved in setting it up, though few of these people were named directly.

Within a few days, the rumors had come to focus on a Washington, DC, restaurant and music venue called Comet Ping Pong, a pizzeria often patronized by Clinton and her campaign staffers. According to the rumors, Comet Ping Pong was the central location for the supposed child sex ring. Facebook posts, tweets, and contributions on message boards charged that the restaurant had an enormous basement where underage sex workers were kept; that sex-related murals lined the walls of the establishment; and that James Alefantis, the owner of the restaurant, was under police investigation for sex trafficking. Hidden tunnels, the stories continued, linked Comet Ping Pong to nearby businesses also in on the plot—the better to whisk children away if government officials came by.

That was not all. Websites, tweets, and message board posts soon provided even more information about the scandal. Posts appeared online showing pictures of children, supposedly taken from the Instagram account of Alefantis. Since Alefantis had no children of his own, many viewers found it deeply suspicious that he would display so many photos of young people on a social media account. Rumors flew that the e-mails of Clinton staffers—notably those of Podesta—were filled with coded messages referring to child prostitution. Even the restaurant's menu, to some, appeared to support the notion that Comet Ping Pong was a front for child trafficking. "Their menu include[s] a pedophilic symbol," wrote a poster on Reddit, "as do the signs and decorations of other neighboring businesses."[2]

> "We're talking an international child enslavement and sex ring."[1]
>
> —A tweet by someone using the name Carmen Katz

The Clinton campaign dismissed the notion that the story—quickly dubbed "Pizzagate" by many in the media—had any truth to it at all. So did Alefantis. But their denials had little if any effect on the rumors. People began calling Comet Ping Pong to threaten Alefantis and his workers with violence, even death. Like other restaurants, Comet Ping Pong was listed on the website Yelp, which offers customer restaurant reviews; Alefantis was forced to close the pizzeria's page, however, because so many commenters were discussing Pizzagate rather than the quality of the food. Nearby establishments began to suffer as well. In a Facebook post, Alefantis explained that neighboring businesses "have reported receiving some spillover abuse as the 'Pizzagate' rumors continue to fester."[3]

Even after Clinton lost the presidential election to Republican candidate Donald Trump, the rumors did not end. On the contrary, many people continued to give them credence. That included some who were closely connected to positions of power. "Until #Pizzagate [is] proven false, it'll remain a story,"[4] tweeted Michael Flynn Jr., the son of Trump's pick for national security adviser. On December 4, 2016, the effects of Pizzagate almost turned tragic when a North Carolina man named Edgar Maddison Welch walked into the restaurant brandishing a rifle and began firing it at random. Welch later explained that he had come to investigate the rumors, which he believed were true. Fortunately, no one was hurt, and Welch was quickly arrested.

The Washington, DC, pizzeria Comet Ping Pong (pictured) fell victim to fake news in 2016 when false Internet stories claimed the restaurant was operating a child sex ring. Responding to the stories, an armed vigilante entered the pizzeria and began firing a rifle.

Technology and Lies

From its very beginnings, the Pizzagate story was not remotely based in reality. There was no child sex ring led by Clinton and her allies at Comet Ping Pong—or anywhere else. Comet Ping Pong was just as it advertised itself—a neighborhood pizzeria where occasional concerts took place, not the headquarters for an international scheme to abuse and enslave children. The tunnels to nearby businesses and the erotic murals on the restaurant's walls proved to be entirely fictional; far from having a basement big enough to house dozens of sex slaves, Comet Ping Pong had no basement at all. Alefantis had never been under investigation by any police force, local or federal, nor had anyone ever leveled any child trafficking accusations against him. And the pictures of children supposedly from Alefantis's Instagram account actually came from other people's pages. Almost the only factual part of the rumor was that Clinton's campaign did frequently order food from Comet Ping Pong. Indeed, the entire Pizzagate story was a deliberate creation. The District of Columbia police department, along with several legitimate news organizations and fact-checking websites, quickly determined that the story was fabricated. They determined it had been made up and spread originally by people—most likely from a white supremacist group, though no one knows for sure—who knew perfectly well that the story was false.

> "Until #Pizzagate [is] proven false, it'll remain a story."[4]
>
> —Michael Flynn Jr., son of Donald Trump's first national security adviser

The deliberate spreading of lies in public life is nothing new. Made-up stories designed to put political opponents in a bad light have dogged government leaders for decades. Abraham Lincoln's enemies, for example, circulated rumors that he was part African American. Opponents of Franklin D. Roosevelt, knowing that anti-Semitism was strong in early twentieth-century America, tried to convince voters that he was Jewish, not Christian. Members of the press, politicians, and civic leaders have consistently used false rumor and innuendo to discredit their opponents and boost their own status. For that matter, even in private life the spreading of unfounded rumors has been used to great effect for years. Countless people have falsely charged their neighbors, family members, or rivals with engaging in affairs, drug use, or criminal behavior, all to destroy their reputations and ruin their lives. In this sense Pizzagate is simply more of the same.

In another way, however, Pizzagate represents something new and different. The story of the Clinton child sex ring is an excellent example of a phenomenon now referred to as fake news. The difference between fake news and the unfounded rumors of another era rests not so much in the content of the lie, but in how the lie is spread. In earlier times rumors such as these were spread through word of mouth, in public speeches, or possibly in daily newspapers; whichever the case, the information moved slowly and reached relatively few people. Today, in contrast, the world is wired, and false information can travel at essentially the speed of light. Facebook, Twitter, blogs, and other social media platforms make the spreading of news, whether true or false, easy and—most of all—fast. Once a distribution list has been created, it takes only a few seconds to share a story with thousands of people via e-mail or social media. That represents a huge difference from 1860, 1932, or even 2000. Fake news consists not just of news that turns out to be false, nor even news that is intended to be misleading, but of deliberately false news stories that are spread largely through the Internet.

Fake news, unfortunately, can have powerful—and in the long run, undesirable—effects. The charges hurled at Alefantis and his employees held them up to ridicule, shook them deeply, and threatened to destroy their livelihoods, their reputations, and even their lives. For weeks restaurant employees were on edge; no one knew whether a ringing phone might be a request for a reservation or a death threat. More globally, Pizzagate may have played a minor role in Clinton losing the election. Some undecided voters may have decided to vote for Trump instead of Clinton based in part on the fake news. But even if the 2016 election was unaffected by Pizzagate, most Americans would agree that elections should not be decided by invented rumors. The possibility that someone might lose because of misinformation is—or should be—of concern, regardless of a person's political allegiance. For this reason, and because the rise of fake news shows no signs of slowing, fake news is a problem for all.

CHAPTER 1

What Is Fake News?

Each January, a committee made up of editors of the *Macquarie Dictionary*, an Australian reference work, identifies a "word of the year." The committee looks for a word or phrase that is relatively new to the English language, was used with great frequency during the previous year, and seems to reflect or sum up the time period. For 2016 there were fifteen nominees, including *standing desk* (as the name suggests, a type of desk at which people stand while working) and the political term *alt-right*, denoting "an offshoot of conservatism mixing racism, white nationalism and populism,"[5] according to the Associated Press. But the committee's choice was a different phrase: *fake news*, or the deliberate spreading of wrong information via the Internet and social media. "The concept of fake news is one of the big issues of 2016," the committee reported, "not only in Australia but around the world."[6]

The designation of *fake news* as the word of the year was apt. Just a few years prior to 2016, fake news had been virtually unknown, both as a phrase and as a concept. In 2016, in contrast, it was indeed of enormous importance. Nowhere was this importance more apparent than in the US presidential race. During the campaign, false news items circulated at a remarkable clip, with baseless claims for or against various candidates appearing on what sometimes seemed to be a daily basis. Whether asserting that Pope Francis had endorsed Democratic presidential

> "The concept of fake news is one of the big issues of 2016, not only in Australia but around the world."[6]
>
> —Editors of the Australian reference text the *Macquarie Dictionary*

Donald Trump and Hillary Clinton prepare for the second presidential debate in 2016. Fake news targeting various candidates was rampant on the Internet during the primary and general election campaigns.

candidate Bernie Sanders (he had not), that Republican candidate Ted Cruz was planning to speak at the Democratic National Convention (he was not), or any of a myriad of rumors related to eventual nominees Donald Trump and Hillary Clinton, fake news was easy to find. Given the prevalence and influence of fake news, both in and out of the political realm, the *Macquarie Dictionary* editors made an accurate choice. Few if any new words, phrases, or ideas were more significant.

Definitions

Defining what fake news is and is not can be tricky. The *Macquarie Dictionary* describes *fake news* as "disinformation and hoaxes published on websites for political purposes or to drive web traffic," adding that "the incorrect information [is then] passed along by social media."[7] Most other definitions agree, at least in broad terms. But nearly all agree that fake news must be not only false but deliberately false. Fake news does not generally encompass well-intentioned news stories that are merely based on incorrect information. In the same way, according to virtually all sources, fake news items must be presented and designed to look like an actual news story. They typically include headlines, are usually written in a journalistic style, and often contain suggestions that the information was originally reported by CNN, the *Washington Post*, or some other mainstream news organization. The power of fake news lies not just in the fakery but in the packaging.

Experts also agree that the online aspect of fake news is central to its definition. Misinformation contained in a letter mailed to a friend or delivered in a lecture to a classroom full of college students is not generally counted as fake news. The material must be distributed on the Internet in order to qualify. That is partly because of the Internet's speed and reach. A single piece of misinformation can be delivered online to millions of people in a matter of seconds; that is emphatically not the case for physical mail or classroom lectures. It is also because the Internet has a democratizing effect. Whereas it was once necessary to own a printing press or a broadcast station in order to spread information to more than a few people at a time, now anyone can produce websites that look as professional as any mainstream media outlet. "For every fact there is a counterfact," writes Kevin Kelly, cofounder of *Wired* magazine, "and all those counterfacts and facts look identical online."[8]

> "For every fact there is a counterfact, and all those counterfacts and facts look identical online."[8]
>
> —Kevin Kelly, cofounder of *Wired* magazine

Not all misinformation that is spread online comes under the heading of fake news. For example, governments sometimes engage in the practice of propaganda, or spreading misleading information about a certain issue or event. During World War I, for example, the British government spread the word that German soldiers invading Belgium and other European countries were committing horrible wartime atrocities. In fact, most of these atrocities were fictional, but publicizing them encouraged British men to enlist in the armed forces and helped convince the population that fighting the Germans was necessary and just. "A great part of the intelligence supplied to us by [the British government] was utterly wrong and misleading,"[9] noted a British journalist after the war. Nonetheless, most observers do not consider government-produced propaganda to be in the same category as fake news, preferring instead to leave that designation for misinformation produced by individuals and less-powerful groups than governments.

Nor does fake news generally include the rhetoric of politicians. For decades, candidates for political office have been stretching the truth, spinning reality, taking their opponents' quotes out of context, and even telling outright lies. James K. Polk, who served as US president from 1845 to 1849, got Congress to approve a war against Mexico by claiming that Mexico had attacked the United States. In fact, the United States attacked first. Ronald Reagan, in office from 1981 to 1989, denied that he had gotten the release of American hostages in Iran by agreeing to send weapons to the Iranian government. The truth, however, was that he had indeed authorized such a deal. And Bill Clinton, whose term ran from 1993 to 2001, lied when he insisted that he had not had an affair with a White House intern. Often, politicians' lies are at least temporarily believed by a large proportion of the voting public. Like propaganda, however, these falsehoods and distortions are not widely viewed as examples of fake news, which again is usually created by people much further outside the limelight than the typical politician.

Parody Sites and Mainstream Media

The intent of individuals or groups that create and spread the information also makes a difference in determining whether the articles they produce qualify as fake news. Websites that describe themselves as satire or parody sites, for example, are rarely considered to be sources of fake news. One of the most famous of these websites is the *Onion*, which routinely publishes stories with headlines such as "Obama Transformed into 20-Foot-Tall Monster President After Being Doused with Job-

While president, Bill Clinton was impeached after it was revealed that he had lied to Congress. Political rhetoric—and even outright lies by a politician—are not considered the same as fake news.

Growth Chemical."[10] In contrast to fake news sites, the writers and editors of websites like the *Onion* do not intend to fool readers into believing that their articles are true. Rather, they expect that readers will accept the articles as jokes and be amused while reading them. Sometimes readers do take joke sites at face value—in December 2016, for example, some people believed an *Onion* article stating that Chicago was covered in 18 inches (45.7 cm) of bullet casings. But the goal of the *Onion* and similar websites is to amuse, not to mislead, and thus these sites do not qualify as fake news.

Finally, experts typically do not extend the definition of fake news to information—even erroneous information—put out by otherwise legitimate news organizations. Every news outlet, no matter how careful or unbiased, is bound to publish or broadcast an occasional story that turns out to be untrue. It can happen, too, that the political biases of the editors or owners of a given media site can influence them to publish or air stories that seem to some readers to be false. Still, few serious scholars consider stories appearing on the sites belonging to mainstream organizations such as *Slate*, the *Atlantic*, the *Chicago Tribune*, or the *Wall Street Journal* to be fake news, even if the stories themselves turn out to contain misinformation.

That is true despite the tendency of some political leaders to dismiss as fake news any news report that paints them negatively. In 2017, for example, Colorado state senator Ray Scott delayed a hearing and a vote on a bill that would have given journalists greater access to public records. When Scott's local newspaper urged him to move the bill forward, Scott accused the newspaper's editors of peddling fake news. "They haven't contacted me to get any information on why the bill has been delayed," he complained in a statement posted on Facebook, "but choose to run a fake news story demanding I run the bill."[11] More powerful politicians can be equally quick to charge that items from the mainstream media are nothing but fake news. As president, for example, Donald Trump has accused media outlets of publishing fake news when they run the results of polls suggesting that Americans do not support some of his policies. Nonetheless, most experts do not consider articles or editorials such as these to be true examples of fake news.

> "They haven't contacted me to get any information on why the bill has been delayed, but choose to run a fake news story demanding I run the bill."[11]
>
> —Colorado politician Ray Scott, complaining about a local newspaper

Lies, Ancient and Modern

Fake news has parallels and antecedents throughout history, though with some obvious differences from fake news today. In Italy in 1475, for example, a priest named Bernardino da Feltre

Mark Twain's Petrified Man

The fake news of the 2000s has many precursors. Among the most interesting of these is a newspaper article written by Mark Twain, one of the greatest American authors. In 1861 Twain, who at that point still used his birth name of Samuel Clemens, arrived in Nevada with the intention of becoming a miner. Within a year he had given up on this goal and had instead joined the staff of the local newspaper.

One of Twain's early stories dealt with a petrified man who had been discovered in the mountains. Though the man had been dead for about a century, the story explained, his corpse had not rotted away. That was because the man had died below a waterfall that carried with it a large amount of limestone sediment. Over the years the sediment had settled on the body and turned it to stone. The stone figure, Twain added, had become quite a curiosity, with up to three hundred people going to see the sight in the first few weeks after its discovery.

The story was a fabrication—and Twain expected that no one would take it seriously. He was wrong. Other newspapers picked up the story, and Twain's tale of the petrified man soon became known as far away as Europe. Twain was surprised by what he had accomplished in fooling so many unsuspecting readers. Though he had originally dismissed the story as "a string of roaring absurdities," he admitted later that the experience gave him a "soothing secret satisfaction."

informed his congregation that Jews living nearby had murdered a local toddler as part of a religious ritual. The story quickly came to the attention of the prince who ruled the region. Like others who heard this information from da Feltre, the prince believed the story. He ordered that every member of the town's Jewish community be arrested and subjected to torture. In the end, several Jews were killed. Not even the intervention of the pope, who did not believe the tale, could stop the carnage. Da Feltre's story, however, was completely false. He may well have known that he was telling lies. Certainly, he had no proof that the story had any validity at all. Yet da Feltre continued to spread the rumor, with appalling consequences for the Jews of the region.

Da Feltre's story points to some important features of fake news, both now and in its pre-Internet form. For one, though the rumor spread by the priest was untrue, it did have a grain of truth buried within it. The toddler in question had indeed disappeared, and some accounts of what happened suggest that the child had in fact been found dead. Thus, the story had a certain ring of truth. Second, da Feltre knew his audience well. Like most other Europeans of the late 1400s, the people of his part of Italy were already poorly disposed toward their Jewish neighbors. They viewed the Jews with suspicion and fear and wished they would leave. As a result, members of da Feltre's congregation were ready, even eager, to hear a message that confirmed their dislike and distrust of the local Jewish population. By feeding into what his listeners already believed about Jews, da Feltre was making his story more credible.

Early examples from America likewise indicate the effectiveness of playing on people's fears and preconceived notions. One of these examples involves Benjamin Franklin, who—among his many other activities—was the owner of a printing press. In the period leading up to the American Revolution, Franklin published rumors that innocent settlers were being scalped and killed by Native Americans working in collusion with England's King George III. Many of Franklin's readers were already inclined to believe the worst of both Native Americans and the British king, so they were happy to believe Franklin's reports. As a result, they became more willing to support a war—which was Franklin's intention in publishing the lies to begin with. In 1898, similarly, US newspaper publisher William Randolph Hearst published fake pictures and stories designed to drum up enthusiasm for a war against Spain. Like Franklin and da Feltre, Hearst knew his audience. He was aware that the average American had little use for Spain or the Spanish and thus would likely accept whatever he published as the truth. From behind the scenes, Hearst was manipulating the public.

Hoax and Imitation

The history of misinformation also includes outlandish and seemingly ridiculous claims that were nonetheless widely believed by readers and listeners. One such incident took place in 1835 in New York City. The *Sun* newspaper printed a series of articles claiming that scientists—led by John Herschel, the world's best-known astronomer of the period—had used a new and powerful telescope to find a civilization that lived on the

Even when stories seem incredible, people often believe what they read. Newspaper readers in the 1830s accepted as true the false claim that renowned astronomer John Herschel (pictured) had discovered a civilization living on the moon.

moon. The articles were reprinted by other New York newspapers and quickly spread to other cities, where journalists republished them as well. In New York and elsewhere, the supposed discovery became a popular topic of conversation, and many readers accepted the articles at face value. "The sensation [the articles] excited was wonderful," wrote Harriet Martineau, a traveler and diarist of the period. "It was some time before many persons, except professors of natural philosophy [i.e., science], thought of doubting its truth."[12]

Hillary Clinton, Fake News, and the 2016 Election

Most pundits believed that Hillary Clinton would win the 2016 presidential election. As it turned out, they were wrong. In the days and weeks following the vote, Clinton and her supporters struggled to figure out how she had lost the race. Among the possibilities they considered was that fake news items critical of Clinton had turned voters against her and handed the election to Donald Trump instead. At first, there seemed to be some validity to this theory. Certainly, fake news received a great deal of attention during the election. Moreover, a disproportionate number of fake news stories were highly critical of Clinton; by most measures, fake news treated Clinton much more harshly than it treated her opponent.

But as time passed and more information about the campaign came out, it became harder to justify the idea that fake news had brought about a Clinton defeat. The data simply did not support the theory. In particular, a study released in February 2017 cast serious doubt on the role fake news actually played in the campaign. The great bulk of voters never actually saw anti-Clinton fake news items, and many who did see them had no recollection of them by the time of the election. Moreover, most voters who saw and remembered the false items were likely planning to vote for Trump anyway. The study's authors concluded that fake news had had very little impact on the race—and almost surely did not cost Clinton the presidency in any meaningful way.

Just as the examples of Franklin and Hearst reflect some of the characteristics of fake news today, so too does the story of the moon hoax. The widespread acceptance of the articles suggests that people are predisposed to believe what they read, even if it seems to contradict much of what they think they know. Moreover, the reports were consistent with the journalistic style of the period. They offered careful descriptions of the landscapes and life forms to be found on the moon's surface: rocks "profusely covered with a dark red flower," goatlike creatures "of a bluish lead color," and a race of people "scarcely less lovely than the . . . angels."[13] They were also written in a sober, journalistic tone, not in a breezy slapdash way that might have suggested a less-than-professional effort. And they appeared in what most people of the time thought of as a reputable news source: the *Sun*, one of New York's most-respected papers. The subject matter of the reports may have been outlandish, but the form the information took made it seem entirely genuine.

Fake news is a modern development with clear parallels in history. For generations, hoaxers, pranksters, and people with a political or social agenda have attempted to use lies to sway public opinion. As the examples of da Feltre, Franklin, Hearst, and the moon hoax indicate, they have often done so to great effect. Long before the twenty-first century, the pieces were in place to make fake news a major phenomenon. All that was needed was an advance in technology—an advance that became a reality not long before the 2016 presidential election. Suddenly, it was nearly as easy and almost as cheap to contact a million people as to get in touch with a dozen. Under these circumstances, the lies of today have become ever more prevalent—and even more difficult to contain.

CHAPTER 2

The Rise of Fake News

Over the past century or so, the world has changed in dozens of ways, large and small. In no area, however, has the change been as notable—or as speedy—as in the realm of technology and communication. In the early 1900s, for example, most American homes lacked telephones of any kind. Cellular phones were not developed until later in the century and were not common until the 1990s. Today, in contrast, cell phones are everywhere. A 2015 survey revealed that 92 percent of American adults owned at least one; similarly, 86 percent of Canadian adults and 93 percent of adults in the United Kingdom were cell phone owners. Television did not exist in the 1910s, and even as late as the 1980s most households could receive only a handful of TV channels. Today ownership of televisions approaches 100 percent, and most Americans have dozens of channels to choose from.

But perhaps the greatest change has been the coming of the Internet. "The Internet has revolutionized the computer and communications world like nothing before,"[14] asserts an article detailing the history of the online world. Indeed, the Internet has brought sweeping changes in a remarkably short period of time. Since the beginning of the World Wide Web in the early 1990s, the Internet's influence has been incalculable. Survey data varies, but only about 15 percent of Americans say they spend no time at all online, and most of the remaining 85 percent use the Internet on a daily basis. Americans routinely go online to send e-mails, share videos, look at pictures, purchase items from stores, check sports scores, read the news, and much more.

Without question, the Internet has added enormously to the lives of the people who use it. Social media sites allow people to keep in touch despite being thousands of miles apart; an astonishing 2 billion people worldwide are members of Facebook alone. Businesses use the Internet to connect with other corporations around the world; libraries make their entire catalogs accessible from any location with Internet access; baseball fans can learn how their favorite teams are doing simply by clicking a mouse. The Internet has revolutionized the way people shop, listen to music, and go to school; at both the high school and college levels, distance learning is becoming more and more common. As a commentator wrote in 2015, using only slight exaggeration, "In today's world everything is online."[15]

The rapid growth of the Internet, however, has drawbacks as well as benefits. Some observers worry about the amount of time people spend online. Web-based video games, social media sites, and other online attractions can divert users from real-world relationships and responsibilities. That is especially true for

The Internet and the many devices that make it possible to communicate with thousands of people in a matter of seconds have enabled the widespread success of fake news. In the US, nearly everyone and everything today is online.

young people. "I have been told that I am addicted to the internet, and prefer its company rather than being with other people," a twelve-year-old British girl told a reporter. "I feel lost without the internet."[16] Children and teenagers who go online without adult supervision can be at risk, too, from sexual predators who try to establish relationships with them. And thieves and swindlers use the Internet to carry out scams designed to fool people into giving up their passwords, credit card numbers, and other valuable pieces of information.

The Internet has also made fake news, as we know it today, a possibility. Until the rise of the World Wide Web in the 1990s, people who wished to spread unfounded rumors and outright lies faced severe limitations on their activities. Unless they owned a printing press, like Benjamin Franklin or William Randolph Hearst, they had no easy way to share false information with others. Sending letters through the mail would have been time consuming and costly; telling people in person would have been inefficient; even spreading lies by telephone would have been expensive and slow. But the Internet changed that. Whether through e-mail, social media, or message boards and blogs, fake news creators of the twenty-first century can make their work available to thousands of people in a matter of seconds—and at little or no expense. These conditions are ideal—and essential—for the success of fake news.

Social Media and Politics

The origins of fake news are difficult to pinpoint, perhaps surprisingly for such a recent phenomenon, but many sources agree that 2007 represents a good estimate. That year saw the blossoming of what at least one writer describes as the "social media revolution,"[17] in which millions of people began to connect with one another across various Internet platforms. Even by 2007 some people were already using social media and other Internet sites to peddle fake news, although the term was not yet in common use. In the summer of 2007, for example, Internet users circulated video clips that supposedly showed UFOs floating in the sky above Haiti in the Caribbean Sea. Though the clips looked like they could have been genuine, they were not; they were created as a hoax. A similar story, also circulated freely around that

A Fake News Creator

In November 2016, shortly after the presidential election, reporters for National Public Radio tracked down and interviewed a fake news creator—a California man named Jestin Coler. In the interview, Coler discussed his motivations for turning to fake news. He had two basic driving forces, he said: money and politics. The monetary aspect was quite straight-forward, Coler told the reporters. Like other fake news providers, Coler earned a small sum every time someone clicked on or through his websites. His sites were visited so often, he explained, that his annual income from fake news was well into six figures.

The connection of politics to Coler's work, in contrast, was complex. The most popular fake news items Coler produced attacked Hillary Clinton and praised Donald Trump, but Coler insisted that he was not a Trump supporter. Indeed, he preferred Clinton. His original plan, he explained, was to use fake news to embarrass the right wing. First, he would publish what he called "blatantly false or fictional stories" written from an extreme, con-servative point of view. Then, Coler continued, he would "publicly denounce" the stories, which he believed would make those who accepted them as fact look ridiculous. If that was indeed Coler's plan, however, it was not successful. Too many people accepted his stories at face value for public shaming to be effective. Fake news, he told reporters, turned out to be more believable than he had anticipated.

Quoted in Laura Sydell, "We Tracked Down a Fake News Creator in the Suburbs. Here's What We Learned," *All Things Considered*, NPR, November 23, 2016. www.npr.org.

---

time, purported to show a skeleton of what it said was a "human of phenomenal size."[18] This story, too, was a hoax.

Once established online, fake news items multiplied rapidly. By 2016 so many fake news items were circulating on social media sites and elsewhere online that PolitiFact, a fact-checking organization affiliated with Florida's *Tampa Bay Times*, awarded its Lie of the Year award to fake news. The news items spread-ing most rapidly and efficiently across Facebook were fake news rather than examples of accurate reporting. Between August and Election Day, the twenty most popular fake news stories had 8.7 million engagements—a term that includes shares and com-ments—while the twenty most popular actual news stories gath-ered just 7.3 million. Fake news stories are everywhere.

The best-known fake news stories typically involve politics. The Comet Ping Pong story about Hillary Clinton and the supposed child prostitution scandal is an excellent example, but dozens of other unfounded rumors about politicians have circulated as well. A 2016 item, for example, told about a campaign rally for Donald Trump at which audience members purportedly shouted, "We hate Muslims, we hate blacks, we want our great country back."[19] This chanting never took place at any Trump rally, but many anti-Trump voters nonetheless believed the story. Another item from the same year, equally fake, asserted that Democrats had a plan to establish the Islamic system of sharia law in Florida.

> "We hate Muslims, we hate blacks, we want our great country back."[19]
>
> —A fake news report deliberately misquoting supporters of Donald Trump at a political rally

Fake news stories focus on areas other than politics as well. Many fake news items deal with the entertainment industry. In January 2017, for example, a fake news item reported the death of television personality Sherri Shepherd, known for her roles on comedy series such as *The Jamie Foxx Show* and as a former host of the talk show *The View.* In fact, Shepherd was alive and well. Others spread lies about business. A 2015 fake news item charged Burger King's British restaurants with selling hamburgers mixed with horse meat. But almost any topic can be the subject of fake news. According to one fake news account, a Missouri teacher tackled a disruptive student during a high school class and then, according to accounts circulating on the Internet, "stapl[ed] his lips together more than 45 times."[20] Again, there was no truth to this story. Nor was there any validity to a story claiming that a man stuck in an elevator killed and ate his wife and children, who were trapped with him, or a tale that fishers in Canada had caught a shrimp weighing over 300 pounds (136 kg). All were fake news.

Fake News Sites

Most fake news stories today originate with websites that present themselves as legitimate news sources. Often the sites have names and addresses that closely reflect those of actual news outlets, the better to fool unsuspecting readers into seeing them as legitimate. One such site, now defunct, used the web address CNNews3.com, and others have addresses differing by only a letter or two from the sites belonging to *USA Today*, *Politico*, and similar legitimate outlets. Thanks to the prevalence of free and inexpensive software, moreover, the great bulk of fake news websites look professional. In the same way that Franklin and Hearst used a familiar format—the trusted newspaper—to lend credence to the misinformation they hoped to spread, so too do fake news distributors of today use the latest technology to begin the process of disseminating their own lies.

Fake news often begins on websites, but the key to distributing fake news involves another part of the Internet: social media. Fake news creators typically use Facebook, Twitter, YouTube, and other such platforms to drive traffic to websites where the fake news can be found. Most often, these creators present a teaser for their stories—a headline or a brief sentence or two designed to intrigue,

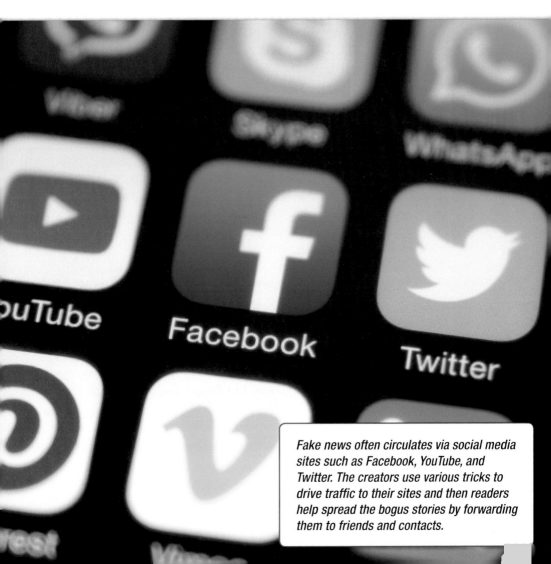

Fake news often circulates via social media sites such as Facebook, YouTube, and Twitter. The creators use various tricks to drive traffic to their sites and then readers help spread the bogus stories by forwarding them to friends and contacts.

Fake News and South Korea

Few countries on earth are as wired as South Korea. Known for its technological innovation, South Korea ranks in the top ten countries worldwide in the proportion of citizens with high-speed Internet access. Smartphone apps are also extremely popular among South Koreans. The reliance on technology, however, makes South Korea a place where fake news can travel at a remarkable rate.

The role of fake news was especially prominent in early 2017, when South Korean president Park Geun-Hye was impeached and removed from office. Fake news about Park and her opponents played an enormous role in the proceedings. Unlike in the United States, where social media drives the distribution of fake news, South Koreans are more likely to share information and links through the use of a phone messaging app called KakaoTalk.

Most of the fake news items supported the president. Some claimed that Western politicians and media organizations were speaking out against the impeachment proceedings. Others provided fabricated data suggesting that Park's support, far from declining as her opponents built a case for impeaching her, actually was increasing. Still others linked Park's opponents to the oppressive North Korean government. In the end, the fake news did not prevent Park's impeachment from going forward, but many observers in South Korea and beyond were astonished at the sheer number of fake news items shared through KakaoTalk—and at the number of Koreans who accepted them at face value.

irritate, or enrage readers. "ISIS Leader Calls for American Muslim Voters to Support Hillary Clinton,"[21] read one such headline widely distributed on Facebook in October 2016. Readers who clicked on the link embedded in the message were directed to a fake news site, where they could read how ISIS, a terrorist organization in the Middle East, had decided that the election of Clinton would better serve its goals than the election of Donald Trump. The story was completely fabricated—among other indications, it quoted an ISIS leader who did not actually exist—but the Facebook headline brought plenty of viewers to the fake news site to read the claim.

Once these links are available on Facebook or other social media platforms, moreover, they tend to be circulated widely by those who have been taken in. Thus, it is not necessary for fake news creators to do much once the story has been picked up by readers—especially if those readers are influential ones with lots of online friends. Users who accept the fake news as real will frequently repost the links on their own pages or distribute them to their own contacts. That is especially true if the links validate the political or social views of the users, either by providing positive information about their candidates or by making bizarre claims about the behavior of those on the other side of an issue. A fake news item implying that Clinton forces had killed an FBI agent who was about to reveal that she was engaged in illegal activities, for instance, was shared over half a million times on Facebook alone and was viewed by more than 15 million people—all in a period of just two weeks in November 2016. In this way, fake news websites can reach an enormous audience with very little effort on the part of the originator.

> "ISIS Leader Calls for American Muslim Voters to Support Hillary Clinton."[21]
>
> —A fake news report popular on social media in 2016

Perhaps surprisingly, not all the people who share the links to fake news sites actually visit the sites. Indeed, quite often social media users pass articles on to their contacts without having read the articles themselves. They see a striking headline, decide that others should know about the situation, and repost without learning what the item says, let alone determining whether it has any validity. According to one recent study, nearly six out of every ten people who share articles on Facebook never open the corresponding link. As a story in *Forbes* magazine whimsically put it, "59 Percent of You Will Share This Article Without Even Reading It."[22] Thus, story teasers on Facebook take on an aura of truth, since so many people come to judge the accuracy of an article not on its own merits, but on the merits of the headline.

Motivation

Throughout history, hoaxers and spreaders of disinformation have most often been motivated by money, ideology, or both. Though it is often difficult to track down the actual creators of fake news stories, most of whom hide behind anonymity, a few fake news creators have been identified and interviewed. Generally speaking, today's purveyors of fake news are also motivated by both politics and cash. For some, the biggest draw of fake news seems to be financial. Website owners sell advertising on their sites, and the amount they make increases depending on how much traffic the site receives. Thus, a fake news creator can become quite wealthy if his or her site is visited by millions of Facebook or Twitter users. By some estimates, fake news providers can make as much as $30,000 a month if enough people visit their websites.

The possibility of earning good money is an especially powerful motivator for fake news providers located outside the United States, most notably in nations where incomes are low and opportunities for wealth are limited. Many fake news providers, as a result, are located in foreign countries—particularly in Macedonia, a small and relatively poor country in southeastern Europe. During the 2016 election, dozens of fake news websites based in Macedonia sprang up. Most provided readers with a steady stream of fabricated articles with a strongly positive view of Donald Trump. But the creators of the sites were generally apolitical. Instead, the draw for them was purely economic. "I started the site for an easy way to make money," explains a Macedonian teenager involved in the production of fake news. "Here in Macedonia the revenue from a small site is enough to afford many things."[23]

> "I started the site for an easy way to make money."[23]
>
> —A Macedonian teenager engaged in the creation and spread of fake news

Of course, politics can be a strong motivational force for some fake news providers as well. An early example took place in 2010, when a group of conservatives in Iowa tried to affect a Massachusetts senatorial election by tweeting misinformation about the Democratic candidate, Martha Coakley. The goal was to discourage Coakley's supporters from voting and to galvanize Massachusetts Republicans and independents to turn out for her opponent, Scott Brown. (Brown did win by a comfortable margin, but it is doubtful that the tweets played much of a role in Coakley's defeat.) During the 2016 presidential election, similarly, partisans on both sides sometimes resorted to the effective if unethical technique of spreading fake news items smearing the opposition. According to US intelligence agencies, a variety of Russian groups, for example, circulated pro-Trump fake news in the weeks leading up to the election. Those agencies believe that at least some of these items were planted on orders from the Russian government.

Dozens of websites registered in the Macedonian town of Veles (pictured) have cashed in on the lucrative US conspiracy theory and fake news market. During the 2016 presidential campaign, these sites provided readers with favorable—though fabricated—stories about Donald Trump.

Whether done for money or for political gain, fake news has exploded in the public consciousness. Though the term *fake news* was virtually unknown just a few years ago, the great majority of Americans today not only know what fake news is but have seen examples of it. The 2016 presidential campaign, which saw an enormous number of fake news items and controversies over whether these items were true or false, indicates just how widespread and significant the issue has become. In a digital age where communication is quick, easy, and cheap, fake news has risen rapidly to become an important part of the political landscape both in America and beyond. Few if any recent trends have had the reach, significance, or controversies associated with the growth of fake news.

CHAPTER 3

Why Fake News Matters

Ever since the start of the 2016 election season, legitimate news sources have produced hundreds of articles and opinion pieces on the topic of fake news. Television and radio stations, daily and weekly newspapers, online news outlets, and political and general interest magazines alike have dissected the phenomenon of fake news from every conceivable angle: what motivates people to create fake news, what encourages readers to believe it, and much more. Chief among these articles are editorials and news items that focus on the question of what the rise of fake news means to society. These articles may be the opinions of a single author, or they may quote experts on journalism, the Internet, or politics. But they have at least one thing in common: Nearly all express deep concern about the rise of fake news and the impact fake news is having on the world. As these experts see it, fake news matters enormously—and the prevalence of fake news today presents modern society with compelling and pressing issues that are far from resolved.

Ethical Issues

The basic reason that fake news matters is simple enough: Fake news, at its most fundamental, is a lie. It is a deliberate attempt to misinform and mislead readers, voters, and citizens in general. And lying, most people would agree, is not a virtue. Most major religions encourage their followers to say what is true rather than what is false. "The Lord detests lying lips," reads the book of Proverbs in the Old Testament, "but he delights in people who are trustworthy."[24] In the New Testament, the Apostle Paul makes much the same argument to his fellow Christians. "Do not lie to each other,"[25] he advises them in the letter to the Colossians. Islam, similarly, argues that those who do not tell the truth are not following the will of Allah, and one of the basic precepts of Buddhism is the promise "to abstain from false speech"[26]—that is, making a vow not to tell lies.

American society in general, moreover, places a very heavy value on truth telling. Those testifying in court are often asked to promise to tell "the truth, the whole truth, and nothing but the truth." Children are routinely instructed not to lie, and old adages such as "Honesty is the best policy" have long been popular in the United States. Indeed, some of Americans' most cherished stories deal with the importance of telling the truth regardless of the possible consequences. One such tale, familiar to many Americans, describes how George Washington chopped down a cherry tree when he was a boy. His father, angered by the loss of the tree, asked young George whether he was responsible. George considered denying involvement but chose honesty instead. "I cannot tell a lie," he explained. "I did cut it with my hatchet."[27] Ironically, the story of the cherry tree is itself an early example of fake news; it was made up by a minister named Mason Locke Weems, who included the story in a biography he wrote of Washington. Though the story is false, the image of Washington choosing to tell the truth has inspired generations of Americans to do the same.

The deliberate telling of lies, moreover, has badly damaged the careers of American public figures. In 1998, for example, journalist Stephen Glass lost his job at a national magazine, the *New Republic*, when it turned out that many of the articles he had written were pure fabrications. More recently, Donald Trump's national security adviser, Michael Flynn, resigned in early 2017 after it became clear that he had lied about his dealings with the Russian government. While some public figures are not harmed much by reports that they have told lies, many, perhaps most, are called to account when their falsehoods are discovered. In general, Americans do not approve of lies or the people who tell them. One significant objection to the spread of fake news is

Americans generally place high value on truth telling. This is evident in the familiar tale of a young George Washington thinking about lying to his father about having cut down a cherry tree. George ultimately confesses after deciding he cannot tell a lie.

simply that the distribution of deliberate lies is in direct opposition to that value. Telling lies is wrong in this formulation; therefore, fake news is a problem.

Harming Reputations

More specifically, because it tells malicious lies about people, fake news is harmful to the reputations of public figures. A fake news item appearing in early 2017, for example, claimed that

Barack Obama had commissioned a sculptor to create a statue of himself—and ordered that the statue be displayed in the White House even after he left the presidency. "Obama Orders Life-Sized Bronze Statue of Himself to Be Permanently Installed in White House,"[28] read the headline on one website that published this bit of fake news. However, the story was entirely fake. Obama did not commission any such statue. Even if he had, he lacked the authority to keep it on display in the White House following the end of his term. The purpose of the news item was to mock Obama and to make him out to be arrogant, pushy, and egotistical.

On the other side of the political aisle, Donald Trump's reputation has been negatively affected by fake news items as well. Early in Trump's primary campaign, for example, a fake news site issued an article about Trump's supposed new campaign logo—a variation of the swastika used as a symbol of Nazi Germany. "Declaring it the 'best, most luxurious, and most expensive logo that any campaign could have,'" read one version of the article, "Donald Trump proudly unveiled his new campaign logo today."[29] Like the story about Obama and the statue, though, the article about Trump and the swastika was a fabrication designed to suggest something negative about Trump: either that he was ignorant of history or that he was willing and eager to link his campaign to the horrors of Nazi rule.

Nor are politicians the only public figures whose reputations have been damaged by fake news. In 2015, for example, a fake news site reported that singer Miley Cyrus had been found dead in the bathtub of her home in Hollywood, California. The report implied that the cause of death was an overdose of prescription pain medication. But the news was false; as fact-finding website Snopes explained, "Miley is alive and well."[30] Another celebrity, movie star and television personality Whoopi Goldberg, was dogged in early 2017 by rumors that she had insulted the widow of a US Navy man killed during a raid on the Middle East. Goldberg supposedly said that the widow was "just looking for attention. These military widows love their 15 minutes in the spotlight."[31] In fact, Goldberg

> "These military widows love their 15 minutes in the spotlight."[31]
>
> —Fabricated quote attributed to comedian Whoopi Goldberg by a fake news site

Politicians are not the only public figures whose reputations can be damaged by fake news. A widely circulated 2015 story falsely claimed that singer Miley Cyrus (pictured) had been found dead in her bathtub—a victim of a drug overdose.

had made no such comments, and the story had originated on a fake news site. As with the stories about Obama, Trump, and Cyrus, the point of the story was simply to cast Goldberg in a damaging light.

Effects on Politics

In addition to being unethical, fake news undermines traditional standards of political discourse. The bulk of fake news items, after all, are negative: They seek to portray political candidates and others in the worst possible light. Since the point of fake news is to drive web traffic toward certain sites, that makes sense. Many fake news providers have found that negative headlines are more effective than positive or neutral headlines in getting people's attention. Even among legitimate news outlets, stories of tragedy, corruption, and disaster tend to have a wider readership than stories about successes. As an old journalistic saying puts it, "If it bleeds, it leads."[32] The prevalence of negative fake news articles about public figures, then, should come as no surprise.

But it can be difficult to live in a world awash in negativity. Nearly all politicians engage, at least at times, in a practice called negative campaigning, which means spending time and money highlighting their opponents' flaws rather than playing up their own strengths. Negative campaigning can be effective, but it comes at a cost. Though research findings vary, several studies have suggested that a relentlessly negative tone to a campaign depresses voter turnout—and could have even more damaging effects on political participation. "Negative campaigning may undermine the legitimacy of the entire political process," reports one study. "Viewers may learn from the mudslinging and name-calling that politicians in general are cynical, uncivil, corrupt, incompetent, and untrustworthy."[33] Fake news, in this way, is much like a steady barrage of negative campaigning and may disengage voters from the political system.

> "Negative campaigning may undermine the legitimacy of the entire political process."[33]
>
> —Authors of a study on the effects of negative campaigning

Moreover, fake news allows for little if any nuance. Fake news items insist that political figures are either good or evil—usually evil—and almost always portray them as self-serving rather than genuinely interested in serving the public good. The situation is made worse because most people only click on fake news items that tend to support and confirm their political biases. Thus, Republicans experience a steady diet of false news items attacking Barack Obama, Hillary Clinton, or former House Speaker Nancy Pelosi, while Democrats see fake news that lambastes Donald Trump, Vice President Mike Pence, or current Senate majority leader Mitch McConnell. As Obama laments, "We start accepting only information, whether it's true or not, that fits our opinions."[34]

Reading fake news items can push people to see only the worst in the opposing party and its candidates. As a result, fake news tends to increase political polarization by widening the differences in opinion that exist in any democratic society. This polarization leads to a breakdown in meaningful communication between people who disagree. In a world where the opposition is evil by definition, it becomes difficult for lawmakers from one party to work with—or even associate with—lawmakers from the opposition. As the negativity and hostility of fake news items drive people apart, political gridlock becomes normal—and the chance of bipartisan action essentially disappears. Few people would argue that this is a positive development for society.

> "We start accepting only information, whether it's true or not, that fits our opinions."[34]
>
> —Then–US president Barack Obama

And as partisanship increases, the impact of fake news increases as well. Fake news items play into the assumption, held by many, that lawmakers from the opposing party are out to destroy America. Someone predisposed to hate and distrust Hillary Clinton, for example, is primed to accept false accounts that Clinton's campaign was funded in part by drug runners from Mexico—a widely circulated rumor originating on a fake news website in 2016. In the same way, a voter already convinced that Donald Trump is the worst president the nation has ever seen will have little trouble believing fabricated claims that Trump eliminated funding for a suicide hotline for veterans—a fake news item from Trump's early days in office. In this way fake news helps feed the cycle of suspicion and hostility. It is a significant part of the problem.

Two Sets of Facts

The divisiveness associated with fake news, however, leads to even bigger issues. Throughout American history people have often expressed sharply differing opinions. That is natural for any country, especially one as populous and diverse as the United States. But it is also valuable for a nation to have a range of opin-

Improving the Free Press

Not everyone agrees that fake news is an enormous problem. Some observers argue that the negative effects of fake news are overblown. As these people see it, fake news may benefit mainstream journalists and publishers in the long run. The argument is that fake news will motivate mainstream news outlets to improve their product so legitimate sources are easier to distinguish from fake news. By emphasizing fact-checking, writer Jay McGregor asserts, traditional news outlets can make it clear that accuracy is essential to good journalism. Thus, fake news gives legitimate news organizations the chance to reinvent themselves for the better.

Others look to history. The world, these experts note, has dealt again and again over the years with hoaxes and disinformation campaigns, and yet civilization has not crumbled. It is even possible to see fake news as a symbol that the system is working. Americans are largely free to speak their minds and publish what they like, and putting up with malicious news articles may be a small price to pay for safeguarding those freedoms. "To my mind," writes business leader Michael Rosenblum, "Fake News is not really a problem. It is rather a function of a free press . . . and that is no bad thing."

Michael Rosenblum, "Fake News Is Not a Problem—It Is an Opportunity," *Huffington Post*, November 28, 2016. www .huffingtonpost.com.

ion on any given subject. When people listen to alternative perspectives, they are given the opportunity to learn and grow. Even if they do not come to change their positions on any given issue, their own opinions are made stronger by considering the viewpoints of others. As one commentator writes, "Healthy, productive discussions are necessary to foster growth, tolerance, and understanding."[35] Certainly differences of opinion can lead to excessive hostility, even violence; but on the whole, honest disagreement tends to strengthen the country rather than weaken it.

Today Americans continue to express differing opinions on an enormous range of subjects. At the same time, though, they are increasingly disagreeing even about the basic facts that underlie those opinions. A recent example comes from sports. In the spring of 2017, Baltimore Orioles outfielder Adam Jones, who is African American, said that fans in Boston's Fenway Park had yelled racial slurs at him during a game pitting the Orioles against Boston's team, the Red Sox. Several other African

American players later confirmed that they, too, had been victimized by racial taunts when their teams visited Boston; one, pitcher C.C. Sabathia, noted that Boston was the only Major League city in which he had ever experienced such abuse. In response to Jones's report, the Red Sox announced that it would crack down on racist language. Indeed, the following day the team expelled a fan for life after he used a racial slur in referring to a black musician from Kenya who had sung the national anthem.

Americans often disagree—even about seemingly straightforward facts. Baltimore Orioles outfielder Adam Jones (pictured) claimed Boston Red Sox fans had yelled racial slurs at him during a 2017 game. Although other African American players confirmed similar treatment, a prominent former Red Sox player publicly accused Jones of lying.

But though many people in Boston and elsewhere were appalled by Jones's claims, others had a very different reaction. Chief among them was former Red Sox pitcher and onetime sports commentator Curt Schilling, who came to the defense of Boston and its fans. Pointing out that no one in the stands had described or filmed the supposed taunts on social media, Schilling denied that there had been any racist abuse directed at Jones. "I don't believe the story," Schilling said flatly. In response, Jones reiterated that his account was not a fabrication, but Schilling refused to back down. "If he wants to maintain the lie he made here," Schilling explained, "that's fine. . . . Adam has an agenda and one needs to only look at his past commentary on race and racism to see it."[36]

Schilling and Jones were expressing different opinions in this debate, but more fundamentally, the two could not even agree on what the facts of the case were. Jones insisted that racial taunting had taken place; Schilling did not believe him. When two sides cannot agree on the facts of a situation, it is impossible for them to come to any kind of understanding. And more and more, conservatives and liberals struggle to come to consensus about the truth or falsity of information. This growing divide is evident to experts and ordinary citizens alike. According to one survey from the fall of 2016, 81 percent of registered voters said that Trump and Clinton supporters "cannot agree on basic facts."[37]

Responses and Ideology

Fake news feeds into this debate over what is factual—and exacerbates it as well. An already divided public will respond very differently to the same fake news item—and will respond in predictable ways. A fake news item originating in April 2017, for example, showed a photo of a badly injured woman in what looked like a hospital bed. "This 7 month pregnant woman was beaten by [a] Muslim refugee in Oklahoma,"[38] read the caption. Reactions to the item differed according to the ideology of those who read it. Readers who opposed allowing Muslim refugees into the country saw the article as true and passed it along to family and friends. But those who believed that the United States should be more welcoming to Islamic refugees immediately dismissed the item as false.

Fake News and Health Reporting

Many legitimate news sites run articles describing new discoveries and advances in the realm of health care. Stories about nutrition, disease, and exercise are often popular in mainstream news outlets; many newspapers and some television newscasts devote pages or segments to health news. Not surprisingly, fake news creators also write frequently about health issues. Unfortunately, the information and advice they give is erroneous, and people who are taken in by the stories may suffer a consequence. In the spring of 2016, for instance, a news item claimed that Los Angeles's tap water had been contaminated with prescription drugs. The story was not true, but many Los Angeles residents believed it—and spent hundreds of dollars on water filtration systems as a result.

Later the same year, Americans became aware of the threat posed by the Zika virus. The disease was real, as was the threat, and plenty of mainstream news organizations covered the story. But so did many fake news outlets. By one count, 12 percent of Zika-related stories shared on Facebook were false. That was an issue, because the tone of the fake news items was much more alarming than the tone of the mainstream reports. The bulk of the fake news items argued that the virus posed a greater threat than officials were admitting. Some charged that the virus was a plot by pharmaceutical companies to sell vaccines. These stories led to heightened anxiety about the disease—and cast doubt on the legitimacy of genuine news reports on the topic.

That, for the most part, is where things stand today: The US population is divided into two opposing sides, each with sharply differing beliefs and an unwillingness to listen to the other. Even demonstrating that a news item really is objectively true or false does little to change minds that are already made up. Indeed, accepting a story as true or rejecting it as false has become a way of demonstrating loyalty to an ideology or political candidate. "You want to show others that Republicans are bad or Democrats are bad, and your [side] is good," points out researcher Sean Westwood. Using social media to spread news items, fake or not, Westwood adds, "provides a unique opportunity to publicly declare to the world what your beliefs are and how willing you are to denigrate the opposition."[39] People are more interested in accepting or rejecting a news item on the basis of their ideology than they are in determining whether the item is actually true.

That is a major concern. The country is potentially at risk if ideology becomes more important than truth and if the two sides cannot agree on what is objectively true or false. A democratic political system, after all, is based on the notion that facts about a given issue are knowable. In this view, voters choose candidates at least in part because they have accurate information about the facts of the issues in the campaign—and accurate information about each candidate's stance on those issues. If voters cannot trust that the information they receive is correct, then making an informed choice is difficult. As twentieth-century scholar and politician Daniel Patrick Moynihan once put it, "Everyone is entitled to his own opinion, but not to his own facts."[40] As many experts see it, people are increasingly feeling entitled to their own facts—and that is a problem for democracy, for journalism, and in the long run, for all of us.

> "Everyone is entitled to his own opinion, but not to his own facts."[40]
>
> —Scholar and politician Daniel Patrick Moynihan

CHAPTER 4

Reporting Real News

Of all American institutions, government is the one most deeply affected by the rise of fake news. Democracy, after all, is at the heart of the American political system. People want to believe that elections are free, fair, and not subject to manipulation by outside forces, yet these ideals are directly challenged by the massive spread and popularity of fake news items. Where government is concerned, the circulation of deliberate lies has the potential to affect election results and to diminish or even destroy the confidence of people in their political leaders. Fake news, therefore, has a particularly strong impact on the way Americans think about democracy and government in general.

Fake news likewise has a powerful—and equally problematic—impact on another American ideal: the notion of an independent press. Americans have for generations championed the idea that newspapers, television stations, and other mainstream news outlets should be unbiased, free from government interference, and focused on reporting the truth. The rise of fake news, however, has had an enormous effect on Americans' opinions of news organizations. So far as media outlets are concerned, most of the impact has been not just negative but downright alarming. Indeed, studies suggest that trust in journalism is disappearing rapidly. In a late 2016 Gallup poll, just 32 percent of respondents said they had confidence in the media's ability "to report the news fully, accurately and fairly."[41] Only a year earlier, the figure had been 40 percent.

For many observers—not all of them professional journalists—this rapid drop is a concern. That is because of the position the news media has held throughout most of American history. In a sense society has traditionally asked media outlets to serve as gatekeepers. In this model, editors, reporters, and producers at media organizations determine which news items are both accurate and important, print or publicize only those stories, and pass the results on to consumers. Of course, they do not do so perfectly; editors and publishers are human, have their own biases, and have often published items that were not at all accurate. Still, over the years, Americans came to see newspapers such as the *Washington Post*, magazines such as *Time*, and broadcast commentators like Edward R. Murrow and Dan Rather as reliable and honest. Not coincidentally, Walter Cronkite, who served as news anchor for CBS telecasts from 1962 to 1981, was known as "the most trusted man in America."[42]

Journalists attend a White House press briefing. Americans have long valued the idea of an independent press that strives for fair and accurate reporting, but the rise of fake news has harmed attitudes toward journalists.

Polarization and the Media

But since Cronkite's day, trust in the news media has plummeted. Part of the reason is the increasing polarization of society. In the 1960s and 1970s, people of all political stripes generally got their news from the same newspapers, magazines, and television broadcasts. Some publications during this time were perceived to have a political bias; the *Chicago Tribune*, for example, was such a strong voice for conservativism that many Chicago-area progressives refused to subscribe to it. Most news organizations, however, played down political biases in hopes of appealing to all potential viewers and readers. Today, in contrast, Americans seem to prefer getting their news from sources with a political slant that matches their own. Conservative talk radio hosts such as Rush Limbaugh are enormously popular among Republicans, but Democrats are much more likely to tune into National Public Radio. MSNBC is watched primarily by liberals; conservatives prefer to get their information from Fox News. As individual news outlets become more extreme in their politics, the image of a trusted news media becomes more difficult to sustain.

Some of the decline in public trust of the media, however, is also a function of how the media has changed. The long history of trusting newspapers, magazines, and television stations was grounded in a sense that journalism was about serving the public good. Indeed, newspaper mottos frequently refer to the national need for an independent press: the *Washington Post*'s current slogan, "Democracy Dies in Darkness,"[43] is a good example. Today, however, the media consists of almost anyone with a blog, a Twitter account, or an e-mail address. It is not realistic to believe that every blogger, every Facebook user, and every person with a website has the best interests of Americans at heart. Nor is it reasonable to expect that these people can—or even should—act as gatekeepers of news, as Cronkite once did.

> "Democracy Dies in Darkness."[43]
>
> —The slogan of the *Washington Post*

Moreover, traditional media is losing its influence. Until recently, virtually all consumers of news in the United States got their information from newspapers, magazines, radio, or television. Today those numbers are down substantially. In a recent survey, just

Anonymous Sources

In the interest of transparency, mainstream news organizations typically identify their sources. There are times, though, when a source requests or insists on anonymity, and in sensitive cases reporters often agree not to identify their sources in the article.

Government employees, educators, and health care workers are frequently forbidden to talk to the media about certain job-related issues, for example. Employees who do speak to a reporter could be disciplined or fired, which is not the goal of the reporter. A similar case might be a person who has knowledge of someone else's criminal activity and worries about experiencing reprisals if his or her name is published in connection with what is happening.

Thus, news reports sometimes include language such as "according to an unnamed source." But though the names of the sources are not made public, they are nevertheless known to both the reporter and the editor. These requirements, obviously, cannot and do not apply to fake news items; it is impossible to adequately source an article that is a fabrication.

20 percent of Americans said they read a print newspaper every day, and the figure for Americans under age thirty was a minuscule 5 percent. The same poll revealed that television, too, is losing popularity, especially among younger people: Less than half of Americans under age fifty said they frequently watched television newscasts. In contrast, more and more Americans are getting their news online—a category that includes blogs, e-mails, web pages associated with newspapers and television stations, online-only magazine sites such as *Slate* and the *Huffington Post*, and social media.

Still, mainstream news sources continue to play an enormously important role in American journalism. Even if only 20 percent of adult Americans regularly read print newspapers, that figure still represents many millions of people—and millions more read online versions of newspapers as well. Moreover, the way that legitimate news outlets report the news provides an excellent counterweight to the practices of fake news creators. To understand the flaws of fake news and the issues it presents, it can be very helpful to contrast fake news practices with the principles, ideals, and procedures that underlie legitimate reporting.

In a 2017 tweet Donald Trump referred to mainstream television and online news organizations as purveyors of fake news. This statement ignores the very great differences between these organizations and those who create and circulate fake news.

Some American political leaders delight in lumping mainstream news organizations in with fake news providers. In a February 2017 tweet, for instance, Donald Trump referred to NBC, ABC, CBS, and CNN as "the FAKE NEWS media."[44] In reality, there are important differences between actual fake news providers and these mainstream organizations.

Sources, Facts, and Errors

For a legitimate news source, the process of putting together a story begins with gathering information. Once editors and reporters have decided on a subject for an article, the reporter talks to people with knowledge of the topic and does research to fill in background information. It is essential for reporters not to rely on the word of an individual person, no matter how knowledgeable that person may seem. As a result reporters generally use multiple sources for each fact. Even a simple story about the opening of a new supermarket, for instance, requires reporters to obtain information such as the store's address, operating hours, and special promotions. The best way to ensure that the information is correct is to use more than one source. Indeed, many media organizations require at least two sources for every fact.

The need for multiple sources is especially important when an article may be controversial or might provoke a negative reaction from one of the article's subjects. Suppose, for example, that a restaurant owner calls a reporter and says that a city official threatened to shut down her restaurant unless she paid him several thousand dollars. The story may be true, but the reporter would be unwise to publish it without looking closely into the details. He or she would need to ask the restaurant owner when and where the conversation took place, for example, and determine whether there were any witnesses. The reporter would attempt to speak with the city official to get his version of events and with people who know the official or the restaurant owner to get a sense of how truthful they are. The reporter would also check city and health department records to find out whether the restaurant has had problems for which the owner blames the city official. If the evidence seems to suggest that the restaurant owner is telling the truth, the reporter and editor will determine whether the information they have is reliable. Only then would they go ahead with the story. Legitimate news sites seldom publish articles unless they are sure their facts are correct.

Despite careful fact-checking and the use of multiple sources, however, legitimate news outlets do sometimes publish information that turns out to be false. In most cases the errors in question are relatively minor—for example, an interview subject's age is given incorrectly, a government official is described by the wrong job title, or a photo caption misidentifies one of the people pictured. *New York Times* editor Clark Hoyt once wrote despairingly of his newspaper's tendency to make small mistakes of this type. "The *New York Times* misspells names at a ferocious rate," he wrote, "famous names, obscure names, names of the dead in their obituaries, names of the living in their wedding announcements, household names from Hollywood, names of Cabinet officers, sports figures . . . and, astonishingly and repeatedly, Sulzberger, the name of the family that owns the *New York Times*."[45]

Making Corrections

Though misspellings and other factual errors like these are generally insignificant, the great majority of American newspapers will publicly apologize for a mistake once it has been caught. Of course, if the error appears in a printed issue of the paper, the mistake cannot be fixed directly, but most newspapers will acknowledge the error in the next issue and provide readers with the information that should have been printed. If the error appears online as well, an editor often makes the correction directly on the website, usually adding a note that an earlier version of the article contained an error that has since been fixed. Many magazines and journals also correct errors of fact. A 2017 issue of a college alumni magazine, for example, included a correction to an earlier article in which an author had placed a chemistry laboratory in the wrong building. "We regret the error,"[46] noted the magazine's editor in chief.

Openly correcting a mistake is especially important when the error in question is more substantial. In 2013 the *Toronto Star* ran a report that a local government official, Margarett Best, had taken a vacation trip to Mexico while on medical leave from her work. The report was accompanied by a picture of Best on the beach, which seemed to indicate the validity of the report. As it turned out, however, the photo had been snapped five years earlier. While on her medical leave, in fact, Best had not traveled at all. The newspaper's editors, aware that the false story had damaged Best's reputation, hurried to express their regret. "The *Star* apologizes to Best for publishing this false information," the newspaper wrote

Mainstream news organizations do make mistakes, but they also publicly correct those mistakes. The CBS program 60 Minutes *issued a correction after it featured a man who falsely claimed to have been present during the attack on the US consulate in Benghazi, Libya (pictured).*

upon learning of the mistake. "We acknowledge that we fell below our standards of journalism in reporting this matter."[47]

Legitimate news outlets also correct egregious errors of fact. "An earlier version of this story indicated that the Berlin Wall was built by Nazi Germany," read an item in the online newspaper *Huffington Post*. "In fact, it was built by Communists during the Cold War."[48] Corrections are typically made as well when interview subjects are misquoted, especially when the misquotation changes the meaning of the original statement. And corrections are used when a source has been found to be lying. In 2013, for example, a broadcast of the CBS program *60 Minutes* featured an interview with a man who discussed his experiences during an attack on the American diplomatic mission in Benghazi, Libya. As

Making Mistakes

A recent example of erroneous reporting by a legitimate news source took place at the end of 2016. On December 29 officials at a power company in Burlington, Vermont, discovered that one of the laptops used at the plant had been compromised by malware. The news spread quickly. By the following day, the *Washington Post* had revealed information that few people had suspected: The machine had been deliberately compromised by Russian agents attempting to gain access to America's power grid. The Vermont hack, in this view, was merely the first step in a much more complex plan.

The story seemed believable, and at first glance it appeared accurate to many readers. The *Post* was a mainstream newspaper with an excellent reputation for getting the facts straight. The story seemed well sourced, too, with reporters apparently getting information directly from US government officials. The original headline in the newspaper's online edition read, "Russian Hackers Penetrated U.S. Electricity Grid Through a Utility in Vermont, U.S. Officials Say."

But the story was false. The *Post* had rushed it into publication without having checked it carefully enough. Upon further review, *Post* editors discovered that the laptop in Vermont was not connected to the power plant's computer network—and so it would have been useless to a hacker looking to infiltrate the plant's information systems. Nor, in the end, was there any evidence that Russian spies had been responsible for the compromised laptop. The *Post*, embarrassed, ultimately issued an apology.

Quoted in Snopes, "Power Play," January 3, 2017. www.snopes.com.

---

it turned out, the man's story was a fabrication. "Nobody likes to admit they made a mistake," the reporter explained, "but if you do, you have to stand up and take responsibility. . . . And in this case, we were wrong. We made a mistake."[49]

Cases of Fraud

Finally, mainstream news outlets also issue corrections when they discover that their own reporters have fabricated stories. One of the most famous examples of this took place in 1980, when a *Washington Post* reporter named Janet Cooke published a dramatic and disturbing article describing the life of "Jimmy," an eight-year-old heroin addict living in the District of Columbia. The article garnered enormous attention and culminated in a Pulitzer

Prize for Cooke. But when it came to light that Cooke had exaggerated her educational background, editors at the newspaper looked more closely at the prizewinning story. It turned out that several editors had wondered whether the story was entirely true when it had been published, but had not spoken up at the time. They decided to question Cooke about the accuracy of her article. When they did, Cooke admitted the truth: Jimmy did not exist. Cooke resigned and forfeited her award. The *Post*, in turn, apologized to its readers.

> "In this case, we were wrong. We made a mistake."[49]
>
> —*60 Minutes* reporter correcting an error

It is important for a legitimate news source to apologize for an error and whenever possible to provide readers or viewers with the facts of a situation. Equally important, though, is trying to determine what went wrong so that similar mistakes will be less likely to occur in the future. "Everybody here takes it to be our first obligation to find out everything we can about why we went wrong on this story,"[50] said *Washington Post* publisher Donald Graham in the wake of the Cooke incident. After significant errors are discovered, reputable news sources pay close attention to their procedures. Perhaps the reporter was too quick to believe an interviewee who turned out to be lying. Perhaps the story was rushed into print before it could be properly verified. Perhaps the editing procedure was lax. Unlike the websites that peddle fake news, reputable news organizations strive to be as accurate as possible.

Aiming for accuracy, of course, does not necessarily imply that news organizations achieve it. Not all errors are found—and not all errors that are located are fixed. Some mistakes are deemed too minor to correct; others do not come to light until weeks or months after the fact, too late to make a correction useful. In still other cases, media outlets are slow to recognize that they have made mistakes—or simply do not want to go to the trouble of acknowledging their errors. According to a study by journalism professor Scott R. Maier, daily newspapers correct fewer than 2 percent of articles that contain factual mistakes. And even if a correction is issued, there is no guarantee that all the people who saw and believed the original error will see the correction.

Still, for all their flaws, legitimate news sources are far more open, transparent, and ethical than fake news sites. Fake news creators, by the nature of their work, have no interest in the truth; they only care about getting their writings noticed. The idea of issuing a correction for a deliberately false article would appear ludicrous to anybody who writes and distributes fake news. To the credit of those who work in legitimate news, media outlets continue to strive to find the truth and present it to the rest of the world. The goal of a reputable news organization is to correct errors of fact—not to spread them further.

Though fake news and real news often look and sound alike, especially at first glance, they are diametrically opposed to one another. Even if a fake news item includes fancy graphics, an appropriately journalistic style of writing, and a website address reminiscent of a major news organization, at heart it has nothing in common with a legitimate news source. The goal of fake news is to trick, ridicule, and spread lies. The goal of legitimate news outlets is to explain, educate, and avoid publishing falsehoods. Fake news aims to tear down and destabilize the country and the world, real news to bring together and to strengthen society. In their goals, their focus, and the way they view their mission, real news outlets and fake news creators could not be further apart.

CHAPTER 5

Pushing Back Against Fake News

"Falsehood flies," mourned Irish satirist Jonathan Swift, "and truth comes limping after it."[51] Though Swift was born in 1667, long before the development of fake news sites, his observation rings true where fake news is concerned. Distinguishing real news from fake news is surprisingly difficult, even for people who in some sense ought to know better. Many people, for example, would say that college students should be well equipped to tell a fake news item from a real news story. For one, they can apply the critical-thinking skills they are learning in school to the question of how to tell real and fake news apart. For another, most college students are what educator Marc Prensky refers to as "digital natives"[52]—that is, they are intimately familiar with technology and social media, having used both throughout much of their lives.

> "Falsehood flies, and truth comes limping after it."[51]
>
> —Irish satirist Jonathan Swift

Yet a recent study carried out by professors at Stanford University revealed that college students struggle mightily to tell fake news from real news. Given an article and asked to determine whether it was reliable, the college students in the study did poorly. Nor did the middle or high school students polled as part of the study do any better. The results surprised and appalled the researchers, who used words such as "dismaying" and "bleak" to describe their findings. "Many assume that because young people are fluent in social media they are equally savvy about what they find there," the researchers explained. "Our work shows the opposite."[53]

It would be unfair, though, to single out students for their difficulties separating lies from the truth. Other research indicates that adults are no better. In one study, participants were given several news items to read and were then asked to sort them into two categories: items they believed were real and items they thought were fake. Most had great difficulty with the fake news items; overall, study participants believed that about three-quarters of the fake news stories were probably or definitely true. For the most confusing item, a fake news report that former FBI director James Comey had put a Trump for President sign in his yard, the number of participants who erroneously classified the item as true exceeded 80 percent.

Recent studies show that many people have trouble recognizing fake news. In one study 80 percent of respondents believed a false report that former FBI director James Comey (pictured) had posted a Trump for President sign in his yard.

The Difficulty of Distinguishing Truth from Lies

Virtually all people in at least some circumstances have difficulty recognizing fake news items for what they are. The reasons why are not hard to understand. People are predisposed to accept what they read, especially when it is packaged in a form that makes it look legitimate—and especially when the content and slant of the news item in question matches their worldview and political preconceptions.

How the information is obtained makes a difference, too, especially where social media is concerned. People typically trust those who forward links and headlines to them. They assume that their friends and relatives will direct them to genuine news sites, not ones that peddle fake news. Once, traditional news outlets served as gatekeepers for news, filtering fact from fiction and presenting Americans with what they needed to know. Today the gatekeepers are no longer newspapers and television anchors, but online friends—and these friends are not especially skilled at the job.

Another issue is that people lead busy lives. They have no time to do their own research to determine the truth or falsity of every news item they see. Nor do they necessarily know how to go about doing this research. And when members of the legitimate media do carry out this research, there is no guarantee that people who saw and believed the initial fake news item will see the debunking—or that they will believe the debunkers if they do. Following the seemingly constant onslaught of fake news items that marked the 2016 election campaign, experts have begun thinking seriously about how best to address the issue of fake news.

Education

For many observers, the solution to the problem of fake news lies primarily in education. Many experts are concentrating their efforts on students in the K–12 school system. School librarians and media specialists have been particularly active in trying to equip students with the skills they need to help them recognize fake news for what it is. Experts often refer to these skills as information literacy or media skills. In information literacy programs, students are taught how to evaluate the validity of sources. "How does the

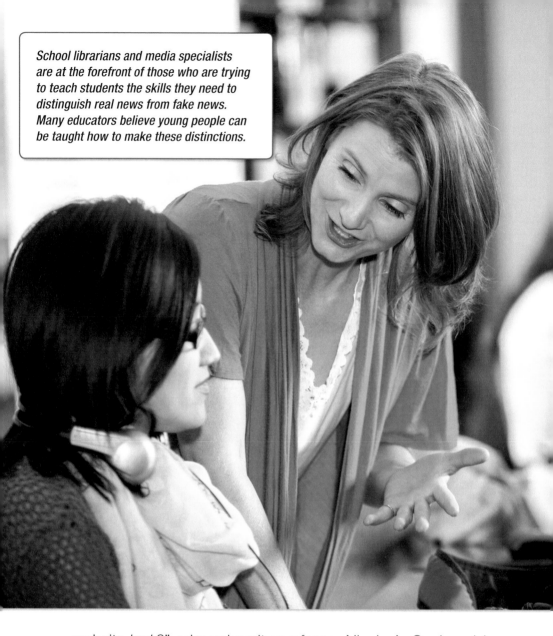

School librarians and media specialists are at the forefront of those who are trying to teach students the skills they need to distinguish real news from fake news. Many educators believe young people can be taught how to make these distinctions.

website *look*?" asks university professor Nicole A. Cooke, giving an example of a question that a school librarian might pose to students. "Does it look like you could have done it on your laptop, or does it look like there's a corporation behind it?"[54] A sloppy looking website, she points out, can be an indication that a site was publishing fake news.

But technology has changed in the past few years, and the rules of thumb that worked in 2010 or even 2012 no longer apply. Today it can be impossible to distinguish a fake news site from a real site simply by looking at its format. "These new sites are so savvy," Cooke says. "The interfaces can be really slick, and they can look a lot like what we consider to be reputable sources."[55] Similarly, information experts could once tell students to look for websites with URLs (that is, web addresses) that include .edu (used by academic institutions) or .gov (government agencies), but that guideline is also more difficult to follow in today's world. Fake news providers increasingly use ambiguous URLs that may end in letter combinations such as .edu.co, but these are not academic websites; rather, the final .co indicates that the site is based in the South American country of Colombia, and the .edu suffix is meaningless. "It becomes trickier to identify these deceitful sites right away," Cooke admits, "unless you're really paying attention."[56]

But many educators are convinced that students can still be taught to evaluate sources and distinguish fact from fakery. The key, these people say, is giving students plenty of instruction—and plenty of practice—in making these distinctions. "This is something children don't know unless we teach them," says Audrey Church of the American Association of School Librarians. "They take what they see on their device at face value."[57] Innovative teachers and programs around the country seek to provide students with tools that go beyond merely looking at the format of a website or noting its URL. For example, students learn to go online and see whether a particular story has been covered by other news outlets. If it has not, there is a good chance that the item is fake news. And some teachers use class time to provide their students with news stories from various sources and have them discuss whether the articles are true.

> "This is something children don't know unless we teach them. . . . They take what they see on their device at face value."[57]
>
> —Audrey Church of the American Association of School Librarians

Fact-Checking

Although most students and adults lack the time and expertise to find out whether a given news item is true or faked, several websites are well equipped to take on this task. These sites, among them Snopes, PolitiFact, and the *Washington Post*'s Fact Checker pages, are collectively known as fact-checking sites, and much of their purpose is to determine the veracity of popular news items. To do so, researchers affiliated with these sites thoroughly look into the articles in question. Where did the article first appear? Who is its author, if an author is credited, and what information can be found about the author online? Can the claims in the article be verified by other websites or reference sources? Once the process is complete, the site posts a description of the news item along with the fact-checker's verdict: a largely truthful news story from the legitimate media or an example of fake news.

One example of how fact-checking sites work comes from late 2016. That fall a story began to circulate claiming that protesters at Donald Trump's rallies were not ordinary Americans worried that Trump might be elected. Rather, the story asserted, the "protesters" were actors recruited by Trump's political opponents, and they were paid up to $3,500 for their work. The story became popular enough that Trump himself referenced it in a speech. Louis Jacobson, a researcher for PolitiFact, however, looked into the story and almost immediately dismissed it as untrue. "It is 100 percent fake," Jacobson wrote, and gave the article a rating of "Pants on Fire"[58]—PolitiFact's shorthand for a claim that has no truth to it whatsoever.

Websites like PolitiFact, however, are not merely interested in assigning ratings to articles that might be fake news. Rather, they see themselves as having a strong educational mission as well. In addition to saying that a story is true or false, they also explain how they came to their conclusion. In the case of the article about Trump protesters, for example, Jacobson explained that he became suspicious when he saw the URL of the site where the story first appeared. The URL was close to that of ABC News's website and looked as though it was designed to fool readers into accepting the item as true. Jacobson also explained that he could not find independent confirmation of the story elsewhere on the Internet. Any further doubts were erased, Jacobson noted, when he was able to identify the person who wrote the article—who freely admitted that all the information was faked.

> "Many times these bogus stories will cite official—or official-sounding—sources, but once you look into it, the source doesn't back up the claim."[60]
>
> —FactCheck.org

Political Bias

While many observers applaud the measures taken by Facebook to limit the spread of fake news, others are less enthusiastic. A few of these opponents dislike any form of censorship and believe that Facebook is infringing on the rights of social media users. Others object on political grounds. Conservatives, in particular, believe that the mainstream media is overwhelmingly biased toward liberalism. They fear that left-leaning media sites will classify news items as fake news not on the basis of the truth or falsity of what the items contain, but rather on ideological grounds. In this view, Snopes or PolitiFact might rule that a poorly researched and badly written article praising the Democratic Party qualifies as real news, while a similar article supporting the Republicans would be listed as fake and removed from the public eye. "Unless the 'fake news' is libelous or slanderous," writes a commentator on the conservative *RedState* blog, "Facebook [has] no business trying to rate which opinions are correct."

Streiff, "Facebook Fake News Hysteria Is Just Censorship and Rent-Seeking in Disguise," *RedState* (blog), December 11, 2016. www.redstate.com.

Indeed, some fact-checking websites include pages where researchers and fact-checkers describe in detail how readers can evaluate whether a news item is fake. In late 2016 an organization called FactCheck.org, for example, posted a page entitled "How to Spot Fake News." On this page, writers for the site offer tips to interested readers. "Consider the source,"[59] the page suggests, pointing out that articles from sites that give no information about their staff members, purpose, or physical location are probably not to be trusted. The page also advises readers to investigate the supposed authors of news items. Just because an author is listed as the winner of a Pulitzer Prize does not mean he or she actually won one—or even that he or she exists. A little research online will often reveal the truth. In general, the page suggests, it is wise to check any claim that does not seem accurate. "Many times these bogus stories will cite official—or official-sounding—sources, but once you look into it, the source doesn't back up the claim,"[60] the article notes.

Fact-checking websites are quite popular. Snopes, for example, receives about three hundred thousand visitors per day. The prevalence of fake news in the contentious 2016 campaign, moreover, has raised fact-checking sites to greater prominence. Mainstream news outlets, political figures, and ordinary citizens increasingly turn to PolitiFact or the *Washington Post's* fact-checking site to help them decide whether a given story is true or false. As fact-checking moves further into the public consciousness, it is entirely possible that the methods and advice provided by sites like FactCheck.org will be picked up by average citizens and used to identify news items that are fake. That would certainly help in stopping the success of fake news.

Changes in Social Media

But perhaps the most important way to fight back against fake news involves social media. Until quite recently, social media sites did little or nothing to discourage users from distributing fake news—even obviously fake news—across their platforms. On the contrary, they seemed if anything to encourage this kind of behavior. Facebook's News Feed application, for example, served as a clearinghouse for news stories that were popular among the site's users. The more popular a story, the higher on the list of items it ranked. The ranking, however, paid no attention to whether the story was true. Thus, the top of the News Feed lists often contained stories that were clearly false—yet despite complaints, Facebook did not act to remove them.

The people in charge of social media organizations had reasons for adopting this sort of hands-off policy. For one, they did not want to step into the middle of a controversy by appearing to take sides in an important issue; like other businesses, Facebook is eager to keep its customers happy. Moreover, social media companies relished their reputation as a neutral provider of services, a reputation that would inevitably change if they took on the role of censors by flagging or deleting popular stories. People in leadership positions at social media corporations were also unwilling to accept responsibility for the role their companies played in influencing the 2016 election. "I think the idea that fake news on Facebook—of which it's a small amount of content—influenced the election in any way is a pretty crazy idea,"[61] Facebook founder Mark Zuckerberg said in November 2016.

Since the election, though, the policies of social media outlets have begun to change. Under pressure from Facebook users, for

Facebook founder Mark Zuckerberg (pictured) initially argued that fake news on the site had little influence on the 2016 presidential election. Under pressure from users who disagreed, Facebook and other social media outlets have taken steps to fight fake news.

instance, Zuckerberg agreed to reconfigure the algorithm used for News Feed to include accuracy in its rankings. Facebook also partnered with Snopes and other mainstream media organizations to help them identify fake news among the links widely shared on the site—and to flag those articles so readers will be aware that the articles are not truthful. Facebook is also permitting users to flag potential fake news articles for others to see. "We believe in giving people a voice and that we cannot become arbiters of truth ourselves,"[62] says a Facebook official.

Concerns and More Efforts

Some experts worry that Facebook's response to fake news is not nearly strong enough. These observers dismiss the notion that anyone's rights are threatened if Facebook cracks down on fake news. Facebook, they point out, is a private company and has the right to monitor its customers' activities—and to set rules

Being Wrong

Over the past few years, millions of people have been tricked into believing fake news items. These people span all age ranges, all ethnic and racial backgrounds, and all levels of education and technological awareness. The first step in combating fake news is to make people aware that they have been fooled. This, however, can be quite difficult.

Part of the problem is that people have ideological biases. They become invested in stories that support their political leanings, and they are unwilling to listen to evidence that indicates that the story is false. Moreover, people do not like being wrong, and they do not like being told that they are wrong. Many people respond defensively when told that they were fooled by a specific fake news item. They may believe they are being mocked for believing the story, and that is an unpleasant feeling. "If you're told, 'Oh, you've been falling for fake news,'" notes a reporter, "it can come off as 'Oh, you're dumb.'"

It is important that debunkers of fake news be very careful about how they approach people who have been fooled. They need to ensure that they do not make anyone feel stupid or make anyone feel persecuted or picked on for their political beliefs. That requires not only verbal skills but also compassion. The combination is not easy to find, but it is necessary if people who are taken in by fake news items are to view what they read and hear with greater skepticism.

Kaitlyn Tiffany, "In the War on Fake News, School Librarians Have a Huge Role to Play," Verge, November 16, 2016. www.theverge.com.

for what visitors to the site are and are not allowed to do. These observers believe that social media sites should not simply flag stories that are demonstrably and maliciously false. Rather, they argue, Facebook has a moral obligation to delete these items and prevent them from being recirculated. For most people, though, the steps Facebook is taking, even if small, are a good beginning and, because of the enormous popularity of social media, may be the best way to address the issue of fake news.

Like social media corporations, Internet providers and search engines have come under attack for their hands-off approach to fake news. In the days following the 2016 election, people searching Google for the phrase "2016 election results" typically found that the first result listed was for a news site called 70 News. Clicking on the site, however, led Google users to a set of fictitious and easily disproved claims about the election. Many

Google users were alarmed that the company's algorithms had boosted 70 News to the top of its listings when it was nothing more than a fake news site. In response, Google agreed to manipulate its algorithm to reduce the chances of customers clicking on obviously fake news items. Google also promised to limit the advertising reach of sites like 70 News. Again, steps like these can help stem the flow of fake news.

Because fake news is a relatively recent phenomenon, it will take time to determine the best way to combat its reach and its impact on society. It will also take time to determine what outcome is most realistic—whether the spread of fake news can truly be stopped, or whether the focus should be on controlling the distribution of fake news and taking steps to reduce its importance. For now, it is unclear which strategies, if any, will prove most effective. Ideally, education will combine with the efforts of fact-checkers, social media companies, and other organizations to improve the situation. But even if the effectiveness of these methods turns out to be limited, it will be essential to try something else and not simply give up. Reducing the importance and influence of fake news is vital to a functioning democracy—and vital to a world in which civility, fairness, and truth are values and not just empty words.

SOURCE NOTES

Introduction: Pizzagate

1. Quoted in Craig Silverman, "How the Bizarre Conspiracy Theory Behind 'Pizzagate' Was Spread," BuzzFeed, November 4, 2016. www.buzzfeed.com.
2. Quoted in Kim LaCapria, "Chuck E. Sleaze," Snopes, November 21, 2016. www.snopes.com.
3. Quoted in LaCapria, "Chuck E. Sleaze."
4. Quoted in Joshua Gillin, "How Pizzagate Went from Fake News to a Real Problem for a D.C. Business," PolitiFact, December 5, 2016. www.politifact.com.

Chapter 1: What Is Fake News?

5. John Daniszewski, "Writing About the 'Alt-Right,'" *Behind the News* (blog), Associated Press, November 28, 2016. https://blog.ap.org.
6. *Macquarie Dictionary*, "The Committee's Choice for Word of the Year 2016 Goes to . . . ," January 25, 2017. www.macquariedictionary.com.au.
7. Quoted in *Guardian* (Manchester), "Fake News Named Word of the Year by *Macquarie Dictionary*," 2017. www.theguardian.com.
8. Quoted in Richard Gray, "Lies, Propaganda and Fake News: A Challenge for Our Age," BBC, March 1, 2017. www.bbc.com.
9. Quoted in Brian Best, *Reporting from the Front: War Reporters During the Great War*. Barnsley, UK: Pen and Sword, 2015, p. 184.
10. *Onion*, "Obama Transformed into 20-Foot-Tall Monster President After Being Doused with Job-Growth Chemical," March 3, 2016. www.theonion.com.
11. Quoted in Bente Birkeland, "When a Politician Says 'Fake News' and a Newspaper Threatens to Sue Back," NPR, February 17, 2017. www.npr.org.

12. Quoted in Lynda Walsh, *Sins Against Science: The Scientific Media Hoaxes of Poe, Twain, and Others*. Albany: State University of New York Press, 2006, p. 250.
13. Quoted in Alex Boese, "The Great Moon Hoax," Museum of Hoaxes, 2015. http://hoaxes.org.

Chapter 2: The Rise of Fake News
14. Barry M. Leiner et al., "Brief History of the Internet," Internet Society, 1997. www.internetsociety.org.
15. Kim Hamill, "In Today's World Everything Is Online," LinkedIn, June 26, 2015. www.linkedin.com.
16. Quoted in "'I Feel Lost Without It': Teenagers Are 'Addicted' to the Internet, Research Reveals," *HuffPost UK*, May 9, 2014. www.huffingtonpost.co.uk.
17. James Carson, "What Is Fake News? Its Origins and How It Grew in 2016," *Telegraph* (London), March 16, 2017. www.telegraph.co.uk.
18. Quoted in James Owen, "'Skeleton of Giant' Is Internet Photo Hoax," National Geographic News, December 14, 2007. http://news.nationalgeographic.com.
19. Quoted in Angie Drobnic Holan, "2016 Lie of the Year: Fake News," PolitiFact, December 13, 2016. www.politifact.com.
20. Quoted in Arturo Garcia, "Did a Missouri Teacher Staple Her Student's Lips Shut?," Snopes, May 3, 2017. www.snopes.com.
21. Quoted in Hannah Ritchie, "Biggest Fake News Stories of 2016," CNBC, December 30, 2016. www.cnbc.com.
22. Jayson DeMers, "59 Percent of You Will Share This Article Without Even Reading It," *Forbes*, August 8, 2016. www.forbes.com.
23. Quoted in Craig Silverman, "How Teens in the Balkans Are Duping Trump Supporters with Fake News," BuzzFeed, November 3, 2016. www.buzzfeed.com.

Chapter 3: Why Fake News Matters
24. Proverbs 12:22, New International Version.
25. Colossians 3:9, New International Version.

26. Quoted in Christopher Partridge, *Introduction to World Religions*. Minneapolis, MN: Fortress, 2005, p. 212.
27. Quoted in Jay Richardson, "Cherry Tree Myth," George Washington's Mount Vernon, 2017. www.mountvernon.org.
28. Quoted in Joshua Gillin, "Fake News Alert: There's No Bronze Statue of Obama in the White House's Front Door," Pundit-Fact, January 27, 2017. www.politifact.com.
29. Quoted in Dan Evon, "Not See Logo," Snopes, November 28, 2015. www.snopes.com.
30. David Mikkelson, "Miley Cyrus Death Hoax," Snopes, September 5, 2016. www.snopes.com.
31. Quoted in Dan Evon, "Did Whoopi Goldberg Say 'Military Widows Love Their 15 Minutes in the Spotlight?,'" Snopes, March 2, 2017. www.snopes.com.
32. Quoted in Aaron Souppouris, "Clickbait, Fake News, and the Power of Feeling," *Engadget* (blog), November 21, 2016. www.engadget.com.
33. Shanto Iyengar and Stephen Ansolabehere, *Going Negative*. New York: Simon and Schuster, 2010, p. 110.
34. Quoted in Matthew Ingram, "What's Driving Fake News Is an Increase in Political Tribalism," *Fortune*, January 13, 2015. http://fortune.com.
35. Becca DiPietro, "There's a World of Difference Between Free Speech and Hate Speech," Center for American Progress, April 21, 2017. www.americanprogress.org.
36. Quoted in Kevin Spain, "Curt Schilling Still Says Adam Jones Is Lying About Racist Taunts," *USA Today*, May 17, 2017. www.usatoday.com.
37. Quoted in Ariel Edwards-Levey, "Trump and Clinton Supporters Can't Even Agree on 'Basic Facts,'" *Huffington Post*, October 14, 2016. www.huffingtonpost.com.
38. Quoted in Kim LaCapria, "Was a Pregnant Woman Beaten by a 'Muslim Refugee' in Oklahoma?," Snopes, May 5, 2017. www.snopes.com.
39. Quoted in Amanda Taub, "The Real Story About Fake News Is Partisanship," *New York Times*, January 11, 2017. www.nytimes.com.
40. Quoted in Steven R. Weisman, "An American Original," *Vanity Fair*, October 2010. www.vanityfair.com.

Chapter 4: Reporting Real News

41. Art Swift, "Americans' Trust in the Media Sinks to New Low," Gallup, September 14, 2016. www.gallup.com.

42. Quoted in Leslie Clark, "About Walter Cronkite," *American Masters*, PBS, July 26, 2006. www.pbs.org.

43. Quoted in James Warren, "The *Washington Post*'s Dark New Motto Is Pure Branding Genius," *Vanity Fair*, February 23, 2017. www.vanityfair.com.

44. Quoted in Mark Follman, "Trump's War on 'Fake News' Is Chillingly Real," *Mother Jones*, April 29, 2017. www.mother jones.com.

45. Clark Hoyt, "So Many Names, So Many Corrections," *New York Times*, August 12, 2007. www.nytimes.com.

46. *University of Chicago Magazine*, "Letters," Spring 2017, p. 10.

47. *Toronto Star*, "Apology: Margarett Best Did Not Vacation in Mexico While on Medical Leave," April 23, 2013. www.the star.com.

48. Quoted in *Guardian* (Manchester), "Oops—the Nazi-Built Berlin Wall and a 'Beautiful' Football Posterior," October 16, 2013. www.theguardian.com.

49. Quoted in CBS News, "'60 Minutes' Issues Apology About Benghazi Report," November 8, 2013. www.cbsnews.com.

50. Quoted in David A. Maraniss, "*Post* Reporter's Pulitzer Prize Is Withdrawn," *Washington Post,* April 16, 1981. www.wash ingtonpost.com.

Chapter 5: Pushing Back Against Fake News

51. Quoted in Leo Damrosch, *Jonathan Swift: His Life and His World*. New Haven, CT: Yale University Press, 2013, p. 210.

52. Quoted in Jeff DeGraff, "Digital Natives vs. Digital Immigrants," *Huffington Post*, June 6, 2014. www.huffingtonpost.com.

53. Quoted in Camila Domonoske, "Students Have 'Dismaying' Inability to Tell Fake News from Real, Study Finds," NPR, November 23, 2016. www.npr.org.

54. Quoted in Kaitlyn Tiffany, "In the War on Fake News, School Librarians Have a Huge Role to Play," *Verge*, November 16, 2016. www.theverge.com.

55. Quoted in Tiffany, "In the War on Fake News, School Librarians Have a Huge Role to Play."

56. Quoted in Tiffany, "In the War on Fake News, School Librarians Have a Huge Role to Play."

57. Quoted in Cory Turner and Kat Lonsdorf, "The Classroom Where Fake News Fails," *NPR*, December 22, 2016. www.npr.org.

58. Louis Jacobson, "No, Someone Wasn't Paid $3,500 to Protest Donald Trump; It's Fake News," *PolitiFact*, November 17, 2017. www.politifact.com.

59. Eugene Kiely and Lori Robertson, "How to Spot Fake News," *FactCheck.org*, November 18, 2016. www.factcheck.org.

60. Kiely and Robertson, "How to Spot Fake News."

61. Quoted in Jordan Crook, "Fake Times," *TechCrunch*, March 19, 2017. https://techcrunch.com.

62. Quoted in David Pierson and Melissa Etehad, "Facebook Is Working to Stop Fake News by Tapping Human Fact-Checkers," *Los Angeles Times*, December 15, 2016. www.latimes.com.

HOW TO IDENTIFY FAKE NEWS

CHECK THE URL

Fake news sources often have names that *almost* match the names of legitimate news sources. Is the URL actually www .cbs.com, for example, or something just a little different?

HOW DOES THE SITE LOOK?

Does the site look as if someone spent time on it, or does it look slapdash? Is the content edited or full of errors?

USE COMMON SENSE

Fake news often makes truly outlandish claims. If an article seems hard to believe, it may well be fake.

SET ASIDE YOUR POLITICAL BIASES

Fake news is most effective when it confirms the reader's own biases. Be especially cautious when reading negative news items about people you dislike.

LOOK AT THE EVIDENCE

Fake news sites usually do not provide evidence for their claims. If they do, there is usually no online trace of the evidence cited in the story.

TRUST THE EXPERTS

Fact-checking websites do a commendable job of determining whether news stories are true or false. If Snopes or PolitiFact says an item is fake, it probably is.

CHECK THE AUTHOR

If the author's name cannot be found elsewhere online, that may be because no such person exists and the article is fake.

IS IT ONE OF A KIND?

If there are few other examples of the story on the Internet, the item may well be faked. Also be suspicious if all the other examples use the same wording.

FOR FURTHUR RESEARCH

Books

Amarnath Amarasingam, ed. *The Stewart/Colbert Effect: Essays on the Real Impacts of Fake News.* Jefferson, NC: McFarland, 2011.

Sharyl Attkisson, *The Smear: How Shady Political Operatives and Fake News Control What You See, What You Think, and How You Vote.* New York: HarperCollins, 2017.

Kelly Carey, *Fake News: How Propaganda Influenced the 2016 Election; A Historical Comparison to 1930s Germany.* Snow Hill, MD: Marzenhale, 2017.

Daniel J. Levitin, *Weaponized Lies: How to Think Critically in the Post-truth Era.* New York: Dutton, 2017.

Internet Sources

Bente Birkeland, "When a Politician Says 'Fake News' and a Newspaper Threatens to Sue Back," NPR, February 17, 2017. www.npr.org/2017/02/17/515760101/when-a-politician-says-fake-news-and-a-newspaper-threatens-to-sue-back.

James Carson, 'What Is Fake News? Its Origins and How It Grew in 2016," *Telegraph* (London), March 16, 2017. www.telegraph.co.uk/technology/0/fake-news-origins-grew-2016.

Jayson DeMers, "59 Percent of You Will Share This Article Without Even Reading It," *Forbes*, August 8, 2016. www.forbes.com/sites/jaysondemers/2016/08/08/59-percent-of-you-will-share-this-article-without-even-reading-it/#61ab0d7c2a64.

Camila Domonoske, "Students Have 'Dismaying' Inability to Tell Fake News from Real, Study Finds," NPR, November 23, 2016. www.npr.org/sections/thetwo-way/2016/11/23/503129818/study-finds-students-have-dismaying-inability-to-tell-fake-news-from-real.

Ariel Edwards-Levey, "Trump and Clinton Supporters Can't Even Agree on 'Basic Facts,'" *Huffington Post*, October 14, 2016. www.huffingtonpost.com/entry/clinton-trump-facts_us_5800e7dbe4b0162c043b6d5a.

Matthew Ingram, "What's Driving Fake News Is an Increase in Political Tribalism," *Fortune*, January 13, 2017. http://fortune.com/2017/01/13/fake-news-tribalism.

Eugene Kiely and Lori Robertson, "How to Spot Fake News," FactCheck.org, November 18, 2016. www.factcheck.org/2016/11/how-to-spot-fake-news.

Craig Silverman, "How Teens in the Balkans Are Duping Trump Supporters with Fake News," BuzzFeed, November 3, 2016. www.buzzfeed.com/craigsilverman/how-macedonia-became-a-global-hub-for-pro-trump-misinfo?utm_term=.ym7XAq53Jw#.frYe4NvRky.

Amanda Taub, "The Real Story About Fake News Is Partisanship," *New York Times*, January 11, 2017. www.nytimes.com/2017/01/11/upshot/the-real-story-about-fake-news-is-partisanship.html?_r=1.

Kaitlyn Tiffany, "In the War on Fake News, School Librarians Have a Huge Role to Play," Verge, November 16, 2016. www.theverge.com/2016/11/16/13637294/school-libraries-information-literacy-fake-news-election-2016.

Websites

AP Fact Check (www.apnews.com/tag/APFactCheck). The fact-checking hub of the Associated Press news agency monitors and explains the veracity of public statements made by political figures.

Factcheck.org (www.factcheck.org). A website affiliated with the Annenberg Foundation at the University of Pennsylvania, Fact Check.org evaluates the truth of statements made by public figures, especially politicians.

Media Bias/Fact Check (https://mediabiasfactcheck.com). A listing of various media sources and their political leanings, sorted into categories such as conspiracy, satire, fake news, and more.

PolitiFact (www.politifact.com). A website owned by the *Tampa Bay Times* and focused on fact checking, especially statements made by political figures and political interest groups.

Snopes (www.snopes.com). An independent website originally devoted to urban legends, but which has expanded to cover fact-checking of statements about the world of politics, entertainment, and culture.

INDEX

PICTURE CREDITS

ABOUT THE AUTHOR

Stephen Currie has written many books for young adults and children. His works for ReferencePoint Press include *Women World Leaders*, *Goblins*, and *Medieval Punishment and Torture*. He has also taught grade levels ranging from kindergarten to college. He lives in New York's Hudson Valley.